MW01383111

Kauai Travel Guide

Discover the Secrets of the Garden Isle – History, Beaches, Hikes, and Waterfalls for an Unforgettable Adventure

Daniel T. Brewer

© **Copyrights 2023 – Daniel T. Brewer**

All rights reserved.

This book's contents may not be reproduced, duplicated, or transmitted without direct written permission from the author or publisher. No blame or legal responsibility will be held against the publisher or author for any damages, reparations, or monetary loss due to the information contained in this book. Whether directly or indirectly.

Disclaimer Notice:

The information provided in this travel guide is intended for general reference and entertainment purposes only. While we strive to ensure the accuracy and currency of the content, travel information can change rapidly, and details such as prices, opening hours, and availability may vary. Therefore, verifying the information with relevant sources is essential before making travel arrangements or decisions.

Additionally, travel experiences and conditions can differ based on personal preferences, individual circumstances, and external factors beyond our control. We strongly recommend exercising caution, using common sense, and following official travel guidelines and regulations. The authors and publishers of this travel guide cannot be held responsible for any loss, inconvenience, or damages incurred due to relying on the information provided herein. Travel at your own risk and responsibility.

Table of Contents

Introduction

Kauai is the second oldest island in the Hawaiian chain, after Niihau. It has the smallest population of any of the islands, with only 72,000 people. However, it is a large island taking about two hours to drive from the northernmost point to the southernmost.

Kauai is known as the Garden Isle because of its lush, tropical landscape. It rains quite a bit on Kauai, which helps keep the island green. This also means it can sometimes be cloudy, with sudden downpours known as "cloud bursts."

When you arrive in Kauai, it won't take long to notice the abundance of chickens scurrying around. While Hawaii is known for its ubiquitous chicken presence across all its islands, Kauai seems to have an especially large population. The reason behind this phenomenon can be traced back to the history of sugar production on the island.

During the late 1800s, when sugar cane was Hawaii's primary income source, a severe rat infestation plagued the old sugarcane fields. To combat this problem, sugar producers devised a plan to introduce mongoose to the fields, hoping they would eradicate the rats.

Unfortunately, they made two critical errors. Firstly, they mistakenly brought in a smaller species of mongoose, which proved ineffective in controlling the rat population. Secondly, the mongoose, being diurnal creatures, were active during the day, while the rats only ventured out at night. Thus, the introduction of mongoose inadvertently exacerbated the rat problem rather than solving it.

Now, you might wonder if the mongoose at least succeeded in eliminating snakes from Hawaii. Interestingly, Hawaii is known for its lack of native snakes. While occasional snake sightings occur due to inadvertent introductions through shipping containers and similar means, the islands are officially considered snake-free in the wild.

So, what do these mongoose eat if not rats or snakes? As you observe the abundance of chickens roaming freely, it becomes apparent that these birds are their primary sustenance. The mongoose feast on chicken eggs, forming the cornerstone of their diet, and occasionally consume chickens when food is scarce.

While the sugar producers initially attempted to introduce mongoose to Kauai, a twist of fate prevented their arrival on the island. The harbormaster tasked with receiving the mongoose took one look at them, shrugged, and unceremoniously tossed the cage into the water, inadvertently causing the mongoose's demise by drowning. Consequently, Kauai is still believed to be mongoose-free to this day. Without natural predators like mongoose, the chicken population on the island has flourished, leading to their overwhelming presence. In fact, the chicken population is so abundant that some people even keep them as pets.

Kauai is an island renowned for its numerous attractions. Its breathtaking natural beauty captivates visitors with its rugged coastlines, lush rainforests, and pristine beaches, making it a haven for outdoor enthusiasts and nature lovers.

Additionally, Kauai boasts an amazing culinary scene that showcases a fusion of traditional Hawaiian cuisine with global flavors and influences. The island's diverse landscape and cultural heritage are reflected in its delectable offerings, ranging from freshly caught seafood to exotic fruits and vegetables.

Kauai is ideal if you seek a destination that combines scenic splendor, thrilling adventures, and delectable cuisine. However, planning a trip to Kauai can be overwhelming due to the abundance of activities, sights, and delicious food options. Deciding how to make the most of your time on the island can be challenging.

I created this comprehensive travel book to streamline your planning process and help you save time and money.

In this book, you will also learn invaluable tips on making the most of your trip without straining your budget. For example, Kauai is steeped in a rich cultural heritage, and there are often free or low-cost events that showcase traditional music, dance, and crafts. By immersing yourself in the local culture, you enhance your experience and discover a more authentic and budget-friendly way to connect with the island.

During my visit to Kauai, I was delighted to witness an abundance of hula dancing and hear the warm greeting of "Aloha" everywhere I went. I made it a point to absorb the culture as much as possible. By actively participating in these opportunities, such as watching the mesmerizing hula dances or listening to Hawaiian music on the beach, you can embrace these enriching experiences at no cost. Not only will it make your journey more beautiful and authentic, but it will also add an extra layer of excitement to your adventure. There are countless creative ways to enjoy the island for free, allowing you to maximize your time on Kauai without straining your budget.

I created this comprehensive travel book to streamline your planning process and help you save time and money.

Let's get started!

Chapter 1: Overview of Kauai

Kauai, the oldest Hawaiian island, was formed through volcanic activity. Referred to as the "Garden Island," Kauai boasts a lush landscape. This abundant greenery results from its frequent rainfall, earning it the distinction of being home to the rainiest spot on Earth, with an astonishing annual rainfall of around 450 inches (equivalent to 40 feet). Consequently, Kauai is adorned with numerous waterfalls. It has served as the backdrop for famous movies such as Jurassic Park, Indiana Jones, and Pirates of the Caribbean 4, lending it an undeniable Jurassic ambiance.

In terms of development, Kauai remains relatively untouched, with only three percent of the island being developed. This leaves vast stretches of wilderness waiting to be explored by those who appreciate the great outdoors. For those who revel in jungle-like environments and enjoy hiking, Kauai offers a captivating experience.

Moreover, Kauai has a unique charm that includes a population of wild chickens and roosters freely roaming the island. These lively creatures are so ubiquitous that a popular T-shirt claims the rooster serves as Kauai's alarm clock. Additionally, the island offers ample opportunities to observe nature, such as encountering honu (green sea turtles) and Hawaiian monk seals.

Popular Highlights

Waimea Canyon

Also known as the Grand Canyon of the Pacific, Waimea Canyon is a vast, 16-mile-long (26 km) canyon with towering cliffs up to 3,000 feet (914 m) high.

Na Pali Coast

This rugged coastline is known for its towering cliffs, cascading waterfalls, and secluded beaches.

Wailua Falls

These beautiful falls are easily accessible and make a great photo op.

Poipu Beach

This popular beach is known for its calm waters and white sand.

Hanalei Bay

This stunning bay is often ranked as one of the most beautiful beaches in the world.

Who Should Visit?

Kauai is an excellent island for honeymooners, couples, and families with older children. There are plenty of opportunities for outdoor activities, such as hiking, swimming, and snorkeling. The island is also relatively quiet, making it a good choice for those looking for a relaxing vacation.

Weather

Before embarking on a trip to Kauai, being familiar with the island's weather patterns is essential. It is common for brief rain showers, known as trade rain, to occur sporadically throughout the day. Carrying an umbrella is advisable for this reason. The temperature fluctuates across different regions of Kauai, ranging from the lower 50s in the mountains to the upper 80s along the sunny South Shore.

The South Shore receives the most sunshine and the least rainfall, while the North Shore experiences the highest precipitation levels. Transitioning from rain to clear skies within minutes on the island is not unusual. Additionally, Kauai can be quite windy due to the trade winds, which reach 15 to 25 miles per hour.

Beaches

Many of Kauai's beaches are not suitable for swimming. Most of the island's shoreline is rocky, making swimming challenging. Consider a few options if you want to swim or spend time at the beach. The North Shore has relatively calm waves during the summer, while the winter months are better for swimming on the South Shore.

Accommodations

Kauai is home to some incredible resorts, primarily located in two main areas: Poipu on the South Shore and Princeville on the North Shore. Keep in mind that staying in these resort areas can be more expensive. If you're looking for more affordable dining options or shopping, I recommend venturing outside the resort areas and exploring towns like Lihuei, where the local population resides. You'll find cheaper options there.

Some notable resorts include the Hyatt, which typically charges around $500 per night, and the St. Regis, which can cost around $700 per night. However, more budget-friendly options are available, such as the Marriott Lihuei, Courtyard, Hilton Garden Inn, and various resort condominiums scattered throughout the island.

Transportation

There is no reliable public transportation on the island, so renting a car is essential. However, be prepared for the condition of rental cars as the roads in Kauai can be rough, with many dirt roads and narrow parking spaces. Due to these conditions, it's not uncommon to find dents and scratches on rental cars. When renting a car, thoroughly inspect it for any existing damages and report them to the rental car company. Also, be aware that Kauai has a significant mosquito population, so remember to bring mosquito repellent if you'd rather not be their tasty treat.

The cheapest gas stations are in Lihue, particularly around the airport area. In terms of getting around the island, one main road circles about four-fifths of Kauai. Although it doesn't encompass the entire island, it is the primary route from the south to the North. The travel time along this route can range from two to three hours, depending on traffic conditions. Traffic congestion is more common around the commercial area of Lihue, near the airport. The speed limits on Kauai are generally slow, with some as low as 15 or 25 miles per hour, so be mindful of speed limits and potential speed traps.

Additionally, be aware of one-lane bridges, particularly on the North Shore. These bridges only accommodate one lane at a time, meaning about six to eight cars pass before the next set can proceed. When approaching a one-lane bridge, yield to any oncoming traffic and wait until the next set of cars yields before proceeding. Patience and cooperation are key.

Shopping

Costco is a popular option for shopping, located in Lihue near the airport. It's a great place to purchase Hawaiian shirts. Macy's, also in Lihue, is another option for finding apparel. For groceries, Safeway is a prominent grocery store chain on the island. If you need a pharmacy or drug store, look for Longs. ABC Stores are a convenient option for various Hawaii tourist essentials and can be found throughout the island. Additionally, the Grand Hyatt hosts craft vendors on weekends, offering a fantastic selection of local goods and arts and crafts.

Food

Many eateries in Kauai are primarily takeout and lack seating. If you prefer a place to sit down and enjoy your meal, check Yelp for restaurants with seating options rather than just a takeout window.

It's also important to know restaurants' operating hours in Kauai. Many establishments only serve breakfast and lunch, closing around 1:30 PM for breakfast places or 3:00 PM for lunch places. Plan your meals accordingly to avoid finding yourself hungry and without any open options. While the big resorts offer upscale dining experiences, be prepared to pay a premium price. One popular tourist spot is Duke's Restaurant at Kalapaki Beach, where you can try their famous Hula Pie for dessert. However, I recommend exploring the local dining scene, which includes Hawaiian plate lunches and Asian cuisine. That's where you'll find some truly delicious and authentic flavors on Kauai.

Major Attractions on The Island

The highlight is Waimea Canyon, often called "the Grand Canyon of the Pacific." It's a magnificent canyon that shouldn't be missed.

Another significant attraction is the Napali Coast, the stunning coastline featured in Jurassic Park. It remains undeveloped and offers opportunities for hiking, kayaking, and boat tours. Keep in mind that you can't access it by car. If you enjoy adventure, the Napali Coast is a must-visit.

Additionally, Kauai offers a variety of adventure activities such as helicopter tours, kayak tours, boat tours, scuba diving, and water sports. Exploring the charming towns of Wailua, Waimea, and Hanapepe is also highly recommended.

Due to the island's abundant rainfall, Kauai is home to numerous waterfalls, some of which you can even drive up to. Don't miss the chance to see these beautiful cascades during your visit.

Hiking in Kauai

Kauai is a relatively undeveloped island, which means there are many excellent hiking trails to explore. If you're a fan of hiking, Kauai is a great place to be.

The Na Pali Coast Trail is one of Kauai's most famous hiking trails. This challenging trail runs along the rugged coastline of the Na Pali Coast State Wilderness Park. Another great option is the Mahaulepu Heritage Trail, which runs along the coastline in front of the Grand Hyatt Kauai Resort & Spa in Poipu. This trail offers stunning views of the undeveloped coastline and the golf course.

However, it's important to note that hiking trails in Kauai are not always well-signed. Bring a map if you're planning on hiking, and don't expect your cell phone to work. Cellphone coverage is very spotty in Kauai.

Here are some additional tips for hiking in Kauai:

- Be prepared for all types of weather. Kauai can experience rain, sun, and wind, so it's important to dress appropriately and bring rain gear.
- Wear sturdy shoes with good traction. The trails can be slippery, especially after rain.

- Bring plenty of water and snacks. There are no facilities along most of the trails, so you'll need to bring everything you need.
- Let someone know where you're going and when you expect to be back.

You can enjoy all that Kauai offers on the hiking trails with a little planning.

Things to Keep in Mind

- There is limited nightlife and bar scene on Kauai.
- Only one main road goes around the island, so traffic can be a problem during peak times.
- The beaches on the north shore can get rough during the winter months.

Kauai is a beautiful and diverse island with something to offer everyone. Kauai is an excellent choice if you're looking for a relaxing, outdoor-oriented vacation.

Chapter 2: Planning Your Trip

Kauai is the northernmost island in the Hawaiian Islands chain. It is the oldest island in the chain and the least visited. Its nickname is "the Garden Isle" because it is the greenest and lushest of the islands.

Kauai is not a big island. It is only about 33 miles wide and 25 miles long. The population is also small, with only about 70,000 full-time residents. Compared to Oahu, Maui, or the Big Island, Kauai is smaller, less populated, more rural, and more laid-back. So, you will be disappointed if you plan to visit Kauai for shopping or nightlife. Hawaii is more about awesome beaches, hiking, snorkeling, scuba diving, whale and seal watching, and history.

The Best Time to Visit Kauai

You've probably heard that any time is a good time to visit Hawaii. And that's true. But there are better times than others if you want to avoid the rainiest season or get the lowest possible prices with the fewest crowds.

The peak times for visitors and high pricing are spring break and the summer months of June through August. If you have a family with kids, this timing might be unavoidable. But otherwise, if you want to avoid the highest pricing and most crowds, try to skip these months.

The winter months of November through February tend to be wetter and overcast. But these are good months for getting some great deals.

Finally, if you want the trifecta of the best weather, minimal crowds, and relatively low pricing, come in September after most of the kids have returned to school, but the winter winds and rain have not yet arrived.

Getting Around the Island

The island is roughly circular, with large impassable mountains around the center. The primary road is a coastal road from the North to the South Coast. But no road fully circles the islands. You can't drive a loop around it.

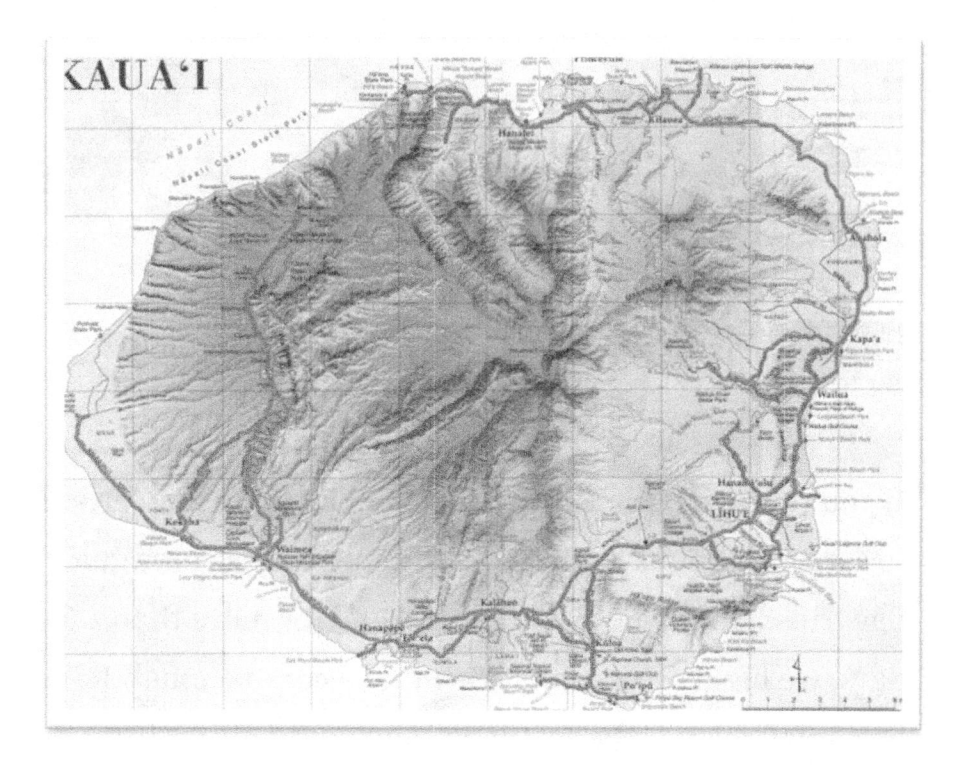

There is just one airport on Kauai, located near the East Coast town of Lihue. The North and east sides of the island are known as the windward side, and they get the most winter rain during the winter season. The south and west sides of the island are known as the leeward side and generally offer a bit more sun and less wind. But really, any part of Kauai is beautiful and has great weather most of the year.

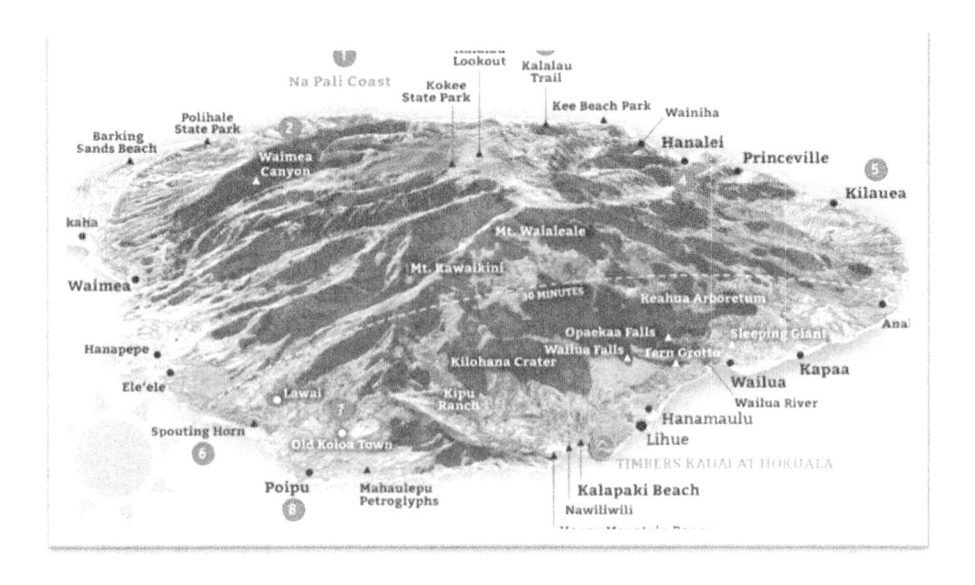

If you're staying for only a couple of days, you may be able to get by without a rental car by simply taking some guided day trips. However, if you're on Kauai for more than a few days, we highly recommend renting a car. Although Kauai is a small island, the traffic is slow, and getting from the very north to the very south of the island or vice versa can often take two hours or more.

As I mentioned earlier, there are tons of chickens everywhere on Kauai. It's funny, and it's unique to Kauai. In fact, there are far more chickens on the island than people, and they just run around freely. Just be prepared to have your share of random chicken encounters.

Where to Stay

There are just three areas to consider for most visitors:

- the Princeville and Hanalei area to the North
- the Coconut Coast on the east
- the Poipu and Waimea area on the south.

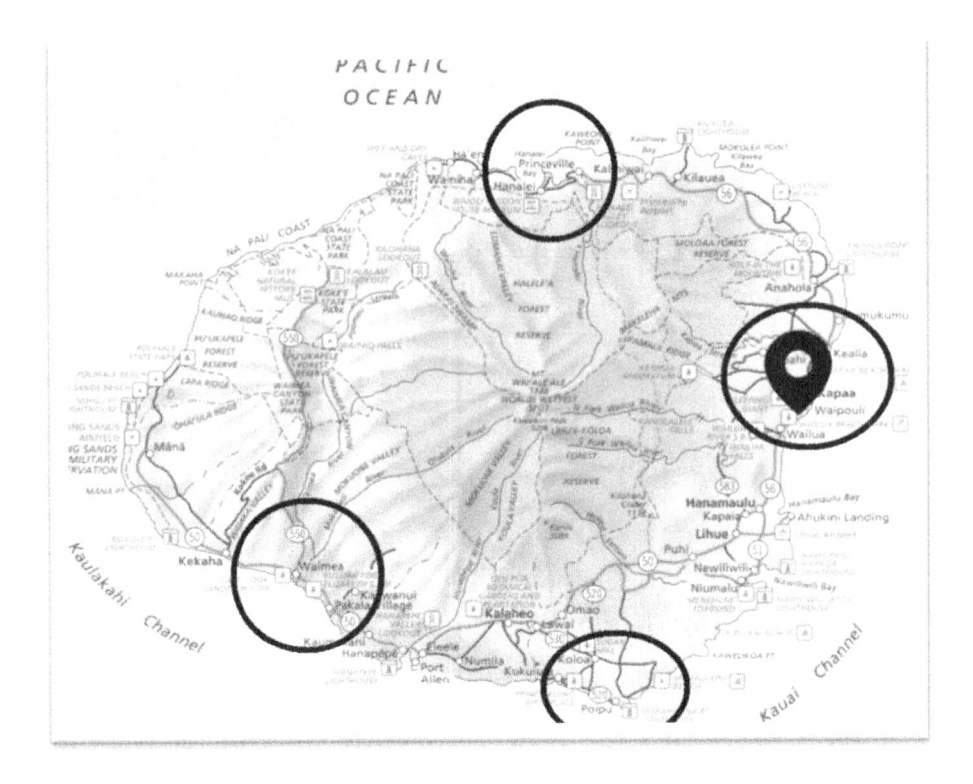

Princeville and Hanalei area on the island's north side is the least developed but has some of the nicest beaches and the best hiking. Most of the lodging options here are small boutique-style options.

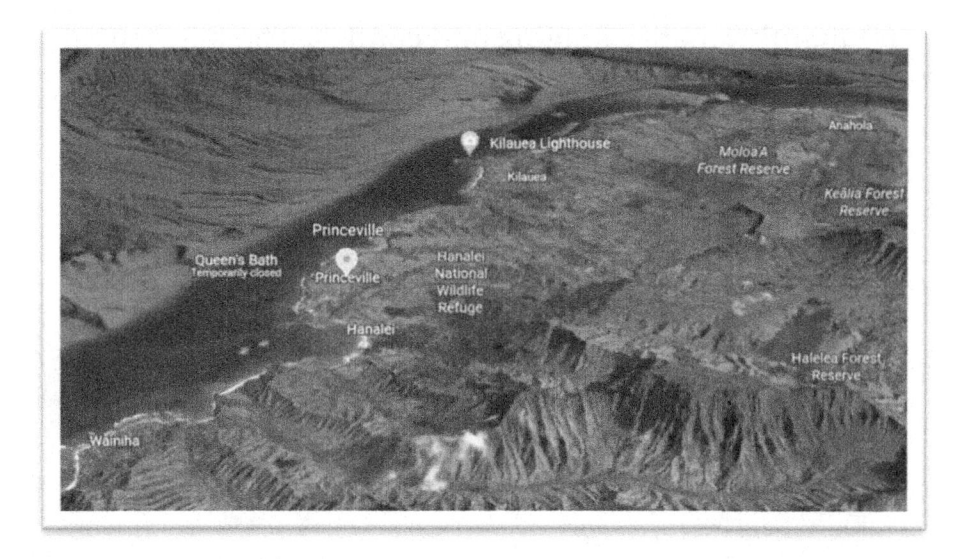

Princeville is a large, master-planned community with big resort and condo options.

The East Coast, often called the Coconut Coast, is another nice option. This area is closest to the airport and the big commercial area. There are a few nicer resorts here, like the Marriott and the Sheraton, but the rest of the options are mainly smaller lodging and condos. The key benefit to staying on the Coconut Coast is that it's the most central location for getting around the island between the North and the South sides.

Poipu and Waimea in the south have the largest resort concentration and are probably the most popular and populated with tourists.

Here you have the Grand Hyatt, another Marriott or two, another Sheraton, and more. There are some nice smaller options here, particularly in the Waimea area.

Finally, a fun fact:

There are no tall buildings on Kauai since a strict building code limits all buildings to the height of the tallest coconut tree. So, no matter where you stay, you'll be limited to either three or four stories high.

Top Things to See and Do in Kauai

The North Shore

Haena State Park: The most popular park on the North Shore is famous for the Kalalau Trail.

Limahuli Gardens: This botanical garden has hiking trails through a rainforest.

<u>Manini Holo Dry Cave</u>: This cave is a great place to explore with the family.

<u>Tunnels Beach</u>: This beach is over a mile long and is great for snorkeling and scuba diving.

<u>Lumahai Beach</u>: This beach is accessed by a short hike through a tropical path. There is a cliff jump here into the ocean.

<u>Hanalei</u>: This town is known for its beautiful Hanalei Bay and mountains. There are several interesting sites to see in Hanalei, such as Hanalei Pier and Waioli Huia Church.

<u>Princeville</u>: This master-planned community has big resorts and golf courses.

<u>Anini Beach</u>: This beach is big and calm, even in the winter. It is a great option for snorkeling.

<u>Secret Beach</u>: This beach is located near Princeville and requires a 15-minute steep hike down to the ocean. There are two sides to explore.

Rounding out the island's north side are Kilauea Point Lighthouse and Kilauea Point National Wildlife Refuge. It has limited hours and requires an advanced online booking.

After this, you start to bend down the northeast coast and come to another beach called Moloa'a Beach. It's another gorgeous beach, but smaller and feels very tropical. Maybe this is why the beach was used as the backdrop for the popular 1960s show Gilligan's Island. For this reason, this beach is also sometimes called Gilligan's Island Beach.

After Gilligan's Island Beach, you'll have a chance to take a break from the beaches and stop at the Garden Isle Chocolate Farm.

After the Garden Isle Chocolate Farm, you're headed down the east coast and coming up on one more desolate but beautiful beach: Paliku Beach or Donkey Beach. This beach has a bonus treat: a cool tree tunnel.

Kauai Travel Guide

Kapaa Town

Directly on the east coast, you'll come to the second town on the island's north side: Kapaa Town. Here you can explore the old plantation-era buildings still in use and some food trucks and restaurants in the area.

In addition to the town itself, there are several things you can do in and around the area. Perhaps the biggest attraction is the Kapaa oceanfront bike path. It's a 10-mile one-way paved beachfront bike path, perfect for walking and biking in absolutely gorgeous views. You can rent bikes around the midway point as you bike north of Kapaa town.

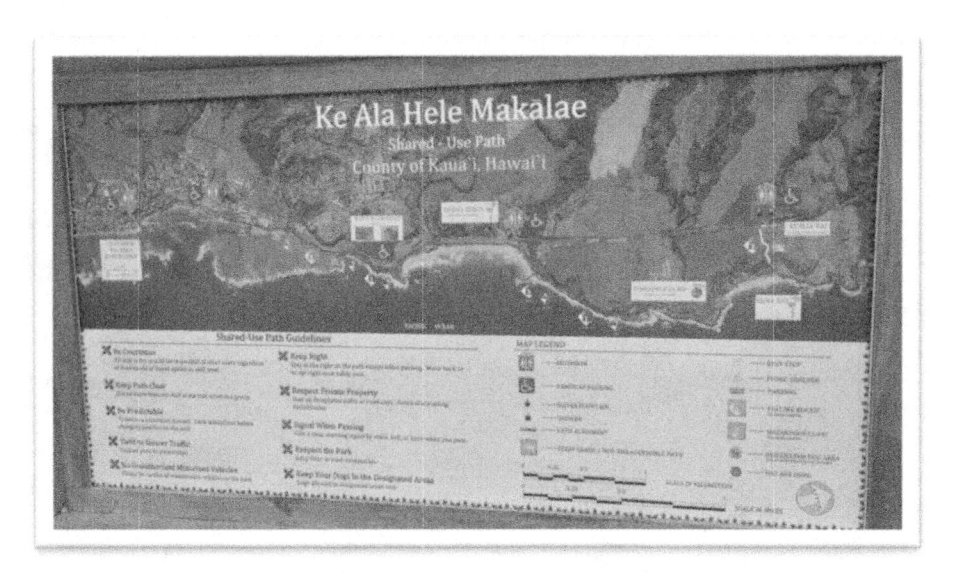

Just outside the town of Kapaa are two great hikes:

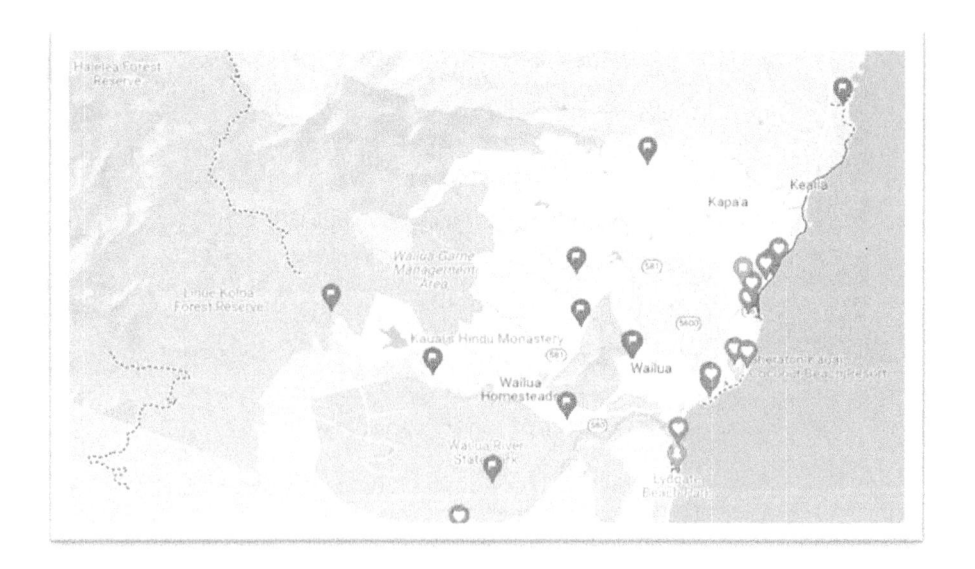

- Ho'o'opu'u Falls is a two-and-a-half-mile round-trip hike through a rainforest to Ho'o'opu'u Falls. You'll hike through the area used in Jurassic Park movies.

- Sleeping Giant, or Nounou Mountain, is a 3.4-mile round-trip hike. It's typically muddy and somewhat steep, so be aware of that, but there are great east and west views as you climb the mountains.

Two smaller beaches near Kapaa are particularly great for small children, with protected areas for young kids to explore:

- Fuji Beach
- Lydgate Park

Both have very shallow and protected water to wade around in. Lydgate Park even has some worthwhile snorkeling.

Two more sites to consider in the hills just west of Kapaa town:

- Another chocolate farm to consider in case you missed the one up North or coming from the island's south side. It's called Lydgate Farms Chocolate Tour.

- A cool Hindu Monastery. Who would think there would be a monastery in Kauai? But it's quite a popular site, and there's a cool story about how it came to be.

We still have the famous Wailua River area. Here you can take boat tours along the river, visit the famous Fern Grotto, rent kayaks and check out Secret Falls.

If you don't want to do an activity directly on the water, you can get in your car and check out two waterfalls:

- Opaeka'a Falls and
- Wailua Falls.

Wailua is a double waterfall and probably the most famous on the island.

The South Island sites

By my definition, the south side is everything below Lihue town, along with the Waimea Canyon sites, which can only be accessed from Waimea town.

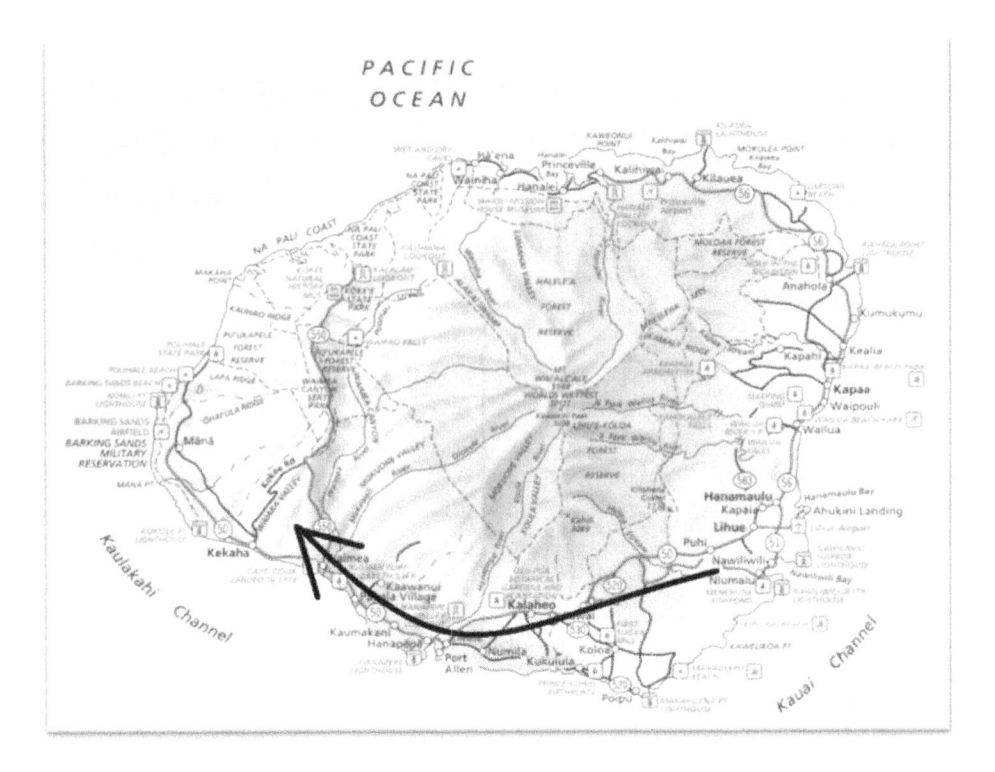

On the south side of the island, Lihue town is first. It is primarily the island's commercial hub, and the airport is here.

Kauai Plantation Railway

The first real tourist site you'll come to will be the Kauai Plantation Railway. Here you can take a guided train ride, nature walks, animal feeding, and try out a pick-your-own fruit orchard.

Next up is the famous tree tunnel on your way to Poipu. It's a mile-long stretch of road with a hundred-year-old eucalyptus trees. It's pretty cool, but it's just a drive-through.

Also, on your way to Poipu will be Old Koloa Town. It's only about two blocks long, but the buildings here are charming reminders from the plantation days, and there are a few shops and restaurants worth considering.

Poipu

Finally, you'll come into the Poipu area and have several sites to consider. Poipu is a tourist village with a collection of tourist shops and restaurants and a concentration of bigger resorts all in one area.

Some smaller beaches are here, but Poipu Beach and Shipwrecks Beach are the most popular.

Travel surveys often rank Poipu Beach as one of the world's top beaches. It's a busy beach.

The other popular beach in this area is called Shipwrecks Beach. There are cool cliffs and a great coastal hike in the area.

To the west of Poipu, along the Beach Road, are a combination of the Botanical Gardens of Allerton and McBryde. Right across the street from that is Spouting Horn Park, which is a popular ocean blowhole. If the tide is right, you can see it blow water into the air and make some noise, but it's fenced off, so you can't get close to it.

Mahaulepu Heritage Trail

The other site here is a hiking trail. But it's not just any hiking trail. It's a beautiful hike along an untouched coast. It's called the Mahaulepu Heritage Trail, about six miles one way. But most people just hike the first two miles to Makawahi Cave. The trail has incredible views, petroglyphs, a tortoise sanctuary, and the last bit of the southern coast, which has never been developed, plus that cave.

About two miles from Shipwrecks, after Poipu, you'll head further west along the southern coast and come to Kauai Coffee Plantation. Here you can do some coffee samples for free, buy some larger coffees, and visit their small museum.

After your time at the coffee plantation, continue west to the small towns of Hanapepe and Waimea. There are some shops and restaurants in Hanapepe to explore and a popular swinging bridge to check out if you have the time.

Then Waimea town is next. It's similar to Hanapepe in that it's a real, local town and probably famous as the starting point for the famous drive up into Waimea Canyon. One popular site coming into Waimea town might be worth your stop: a Russian fort.

Waimea Canyon Drive and the Napali Coast

Next up is Waimea Canyon Drive and the Napali Coast. This is perhaps the biggest single attraction on Kauai Island, and this drive and its associated sites will take you a good full day, particularly if you do a decent hike. Waimea Canyon is sometimes called the Grand Canyon of the Pacific, and some of its views are quite incredible.

The Waimea Canyon and Napali Coast experience is a 38-mile round-trip drive up into a canyon area on the southwest side of the island. There are several breathtaking viewpoints along the drive and many hiking options. And at the end, there are great views out over the rugged Napali Coast.

Pro tip:

There's only one place to stop for food or drink along the entire drive: the Koke'e Lodge, almost at the end of the road. So, it's probably best to bring some extra water and snacks with you.

Here are just a few of the things to see and do along this drive:

- As mentioned earlier, there are numerous incredible lookout points along the drive, but visiting some of them costs money, so be aware of that.

- There's a Red Dirt Waterfall, a popular stop, and it is pretty cool.

- There's also an Iliau Nature Loop. This is a short half-mile walk along a ridge of the canyon with some interpretive signs about local plants and animals. This is the shortest hike you can do along this drive, and it's probably something everyone should stop and do.

But in addition to this very short hike, there are more than a dozen very popular hikes to consider along this drive.

You'll come to Koke'e State Park toward the end of the drive. There's a small museum, some kid-friendly trails, and the only place along this trip for a bite to eat at the Koke'e Lodge.

Then, at the very end of the road, there are a couple of awesome lookouts to the west and a trailhead into the rugged Napali Coast.

After seeing what you wanted at the end of the road, it's time to turn around and head back down, stopping at whatever sites you missed on the way up.

Some Popular Guided and Group Excursions

Whale-watching and snorkeling tours.

Kauai is a prime destination for whale watchers, especially humpbacks in winter, with December through April being the peak.

Na Pali Coast tours

Also extremely popular, but also very expensive, are Napali Coast tours, either by boat or helicopter. Many companies offer these tours, so shop around and maybe look for a coupon to keep the price down as best you can.

Luau

One can't visit Hawaii without attending at least one luau, right? There are three primary options around Kauai for you to consider: Tahiti Nui in Hanalei in the North, Smith Family Luau near Kapaa town on the east coast, and the Grand Hyatt Luau in Poipu on the South.

Kayaking

If you want something a little bit cheaper, horseback rides, bike rides, river kayaking, and stand-up paddle boards on local rivers are also very popular and some of the least expensive group tours.

Chapter 3: Exploring the Beauty of Kauai

Kauai is one of the Hawaiian Islands, all of which are volcanic in origin. But Kauai is unique. It's not as touristy as other main islands like Oahu or Maui, but it is the oldest island in the Hawaiian island chain.

Kauai is the fourth largest Hawaiian island and is over 5 million years old, making it the oldest of the Big Islands. Kauai sits northeast of Oahu, and the main airport, which you'll probably be flying in and out of, is in the south of the island in a town called Lihue.

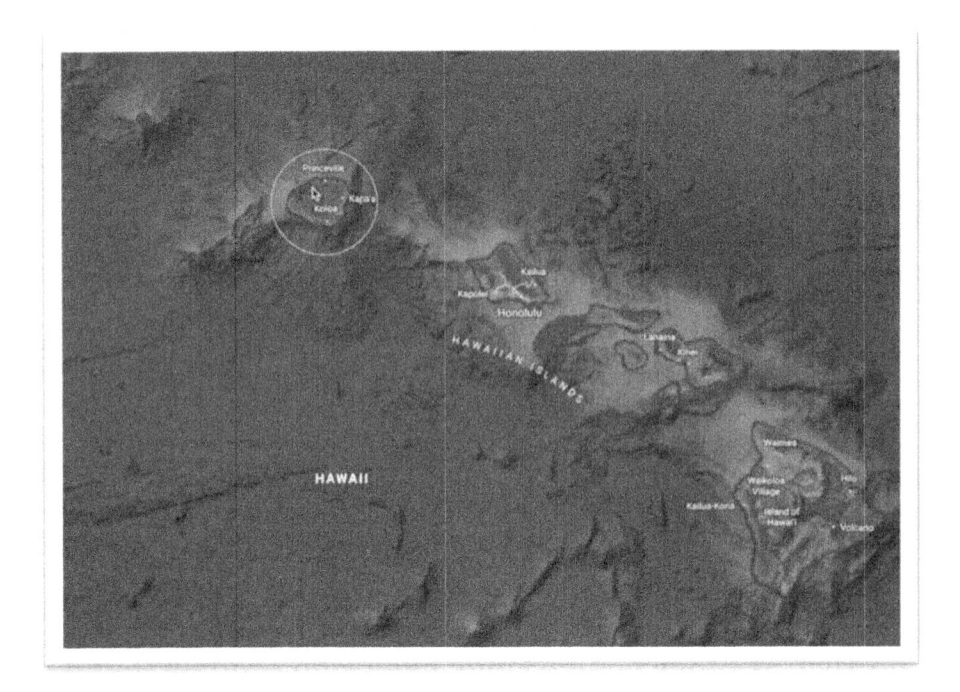

The island's origins are volcanic, and because it's the oldest island, it has the most sandy beaches in Hawaii.

Kauai's Different Ecosystems

Kauai is stunning no matter where you are on the island, but the island has very distinct ecosystems. And depending on what you're looking for will influence where you choose to stay.

North Shore

The island's North Shore is perhaps the most scenic. It's absolutely beautiful. The Napa li coast is a rugged coastline of large mountains jutting into the sea. The only way to get in there is on foot on the Napa li Coast Trail. It's a multiple-day hike with backpacking where you have to camp. It is very popular, so you must book about a year in advance to get your reservations. And you would have to do that through the Hawaiian Parks website.

If you're into surfing, then check out Hanalei Bay. It's one of the best waves on the island. If you're into surfing, look into staying in Princeville.

East Shore

The east shore is one of the most popular regions in Kauai. It's the island's main hub, littered with idyllic, beautiful beaches, coconut palms lined on the sand, and plenty of places for swimming, surfing, and snorkeling.

More Things to Do in Kauai

There are so many things to do in Kauai:

Hiking:

Kauai is a hiker's paradise. There are trails to suit all experience levels, from the easy Alakai Swamp Trail to the challenging Kalalau Trail.

Water activities:

Kauai is surrounded by water, so it's no surprise that there are many water activities to enjoy. Go surfing, stand-up paddleboarding, kayaking, or snorkeling. You can even take a boat tour to see the Na Pali Coast.

Visiting historical sites:

Kauai has a rich history, dating back to the days of the early Polynesians. There are several historical sites to visit, including the Waimea Canyon.

The East Coast

The East Coast is known as the "Coconut Coast" and is home to three of Kauai's most popular tourist destinations: Kapaa, Wailua, and Hanalei. Not only is this eastern coast quite central, with many options for accommodation, but it's also pretty safe to get in the water for swimming and snorkeling. And there are so many activities to choose from, including one of the coolest things in Kauai: renting a kayak and paddling up the Wailua River.

The South Shore is a good spot to be centrally located between the East and West Coasts. However, finding accommodation here is a little bit more difficult because there aren't as many options.

The West Coast

The Waimea Canyon is nicknamed the "Grand Canyon of the Pacific." It is an absolutely stunning natural formation. The canyon is tropical but volcanic, which creates a very interesting combination of flora and fauna.

- The Waimea Canyon gets to quite a high elevation, so be prepared for the temperature difference. The temperature at the top will be way different than the beach's temperature. Ensure you have a rain jacket or a windbreaker to keep warm. Waimea Canyon was one of the most beautiful places I've ever been.

- There are tons of different options for hikes in the Waimea Canyon. If you're looking for hikes in the area, I recommend downloading an app called 'AllTrails.' It's essentially an app that you can download and allows you to find hikes in your area.

- So, if you're going to hike down into the Waimea Canyon, ensure you're prepared. Make sure that you have the right footwear. The terrain there is not designed for flip-flops. You may not think to bring hiking boots to Hawaii or Kauai, but it's a good call.

- And bring at least 2-3 liters of water. It can get hot down there. And food, because it's easy going down, but you know the halfway point where you turn around, you have to hike back out of the canyon. So just be prepared.

Alongside Waimea Canyon, you also have Koke'e State Park, another beautiful state park on the island's west coast. Camping is permitted there.

The weather on the island is pretty stable throughout the year. It's always quite pleasant but just be prepared for tropical weather. So, there's a lot of humidity. Also, the sun is quite strong, so be prepared to protect your skin. And also bring a rain jacket and an umbrella because it rains quite a lot.

Mount Waialeale

Mount Waialeale, the second tallest point on the island of Kauai, is often called the wettest place on Earth. That's why it's called Garden Island.

Beaches

Hawaii is home to countless beautiful beaches, and honestly, pretty much anywhere you go on the island, you're going to find beautiful beaches.

Poipu Beach

Poipu Beach is one of the most popular spots on the island but for a good reason. It's often been named the best beach in the world and is always on the list of the best beaches in the country. Located on the south side of Kauai, Poipu is often nicknamed the "sunny side of paradise," with plenty of activities for sun and sand.

This is a great place to go if you're into seeing Hawaiian wildlife in the wild. You have seals, whales, and dolphins, but the giant sea turtles are probably most likely to steal your attention.

The Queen's Bath

Another unique destination in the Hanalei area is the Queen's Bath. It used to be only open to the alii, or the royalty, the hereditary rulers of Hawaii. The waters were considered sacred, and it was an area where the royalty could come and bathe and wash away their stress. Now it's open to the public, but you must be careful.

The tidepool is quite dangerous. People jump in and swim, but there are very strong currents and big waves. The big surf can push the water right up against the rock. So, if you come to the Queen's Bath, be careful. I highly recommend that you don't go swimming. Also, make sure that you're wearing proper footwear. The trail down to the Queen's Bath was extremely wet, slippery, and muddy.

Food

When visiting Hawaii, make sure that you sample the local cuisine. Food trucks are a great way to sample the cuisine of Kauai without breaking the bank. And Kapaa is the best place to go if you're looking for food trucks. No visit to

Kauai would be complete without sampling some poke. Poke has skyrocketed in popularity worldwide, but this Native Hawaiian dish is best sampled in the local markets.

If you want more history and heritage, I highly recommend checking out the Koloa Heritage Trail. Located in the historic town of Kapaa, the heritage trail takes you past sugar and pineapple plantations that date back to the mid-1800s. And Spouting Horn Park, home to Kauai's famous blowhole.

I recommend exploring the history and culture of Hawaii's legendary grounds. Just a short drive from Hanalei sits one of Kauai's most notable areas famous in Hawaiian folklore. The Menehune fish pond is storied to have been built hundreds of years ago in one night by the mythical Menehune people.

The legend isn't the only thing that makes this landmark unique – it also has many endangered bird species in the Waimea National Wildlife Refuge. Kauai is also rumored to be the birthplace of the Hawaiian hula dance.

Historical Sites

Kauai is nicknamed "The Garden Isle" because this island is very lush and green. This island gets the most amount of rainfall. The mountains of Kauai are the wettest spot on this entire planet. They get more rain than anywhere else on Earth!

Kauai is also the most northern island you can visit, apart from Niihau, known as "The Forbidden Isle."

The Story of Captain Cook

The island of Kauai is where Captain Cook first arrived, becoming one of the earliest Westerners to discover Hawaii along with his men. Hailing from England, Captain Cook was an esteemed explorer with a prominent status.

Upon his arrival on Kauai, Captain Cook was revered and treated as a god. This was because he coincided with the season of Lono, a significant deity in Hawaiian mythology associated with agriculture and fertility. The Hawaiian belief held that Lono would emerge from the ocean bearing white cloths, a depiction that aligned with Captain Cook's arrival on a sail ship with white sails. Consequently, the Hawaiians naturally assumed him to be Lono and bestowed upon him divine reverence.

However, Captain Cook's primary objective was to explore the challenging Bering Sea. Yet, the harsh conditions caused damage to his ship, necessitating repairs and a return to Hawaii. On his second arrival, he landed on the Big Island during the season of Ku, the god associated with war. This time, the reception from the Hawaiians was less amiable, partly due to their realization of the detrimental effects of Captain Cook's presence.

Hawaii's isolated location in the vast Pacific Ocean meant that the ancient Hawaiians lacked immunity to diseases prevalent elsewhere. Even common ailments like the common cold posed a significant threat to them. Consequently, when Captain Cook and his men arrived, they inadvertently introduced diseases that ravaged the vulnerable Hawaiian population. When Captain Cook returned for his second visit, these diseases had already spread throughout the islands.

Aware of the correlation between Captain Cook's arrival and the devastating consequences of the introduced diseases, the Hawaiians recognized his detrimental impact on their people. This understanding was the primary reason for their changed attitude and lack of hospitality during his second visit.

One night, while Captain Cook and his men slept on the Big Island, a group of Hawaiians stealthily boarded his ship and seized several longboats. These longboats were used to ferry individuals from the ship to the beach and held valuable nails. Nails were a prized commodity in Hawaii, as they were affixed to clubs to create weapons. This act was motivated by the season of Ku, associated with war and conflict.

When Captain Cook awoke to discover the missing longboats, he grew furious and confronted the Hawaiians. However, it was too late, as the Hawaiians had burned down the longboats to retrieve the precious nails. Burning the boats ensured that only the nails remained amidst the ashes.

Enraged by the loss of his longboats, Captain Cook engaged in a skirmish with his men and the ancient Hawaiians on the beach of the Big Island. During the altercation, a Hawaiian warrior brandished a spear and declared, "If this guy is really Lono, nothing should happen when I chuck this spear at him." True to his words, the spear pierced Captain Cook, sealing his fate.

Chapter 4: A Food Lover's Guide to the Island

Puka Dogs

You might not think about eating hot dogs when you visit Hawaii, but let me tell you, this isn't an average hot dog. This is a truly unique Hawaii hot dog experience. They also have veggie hot dogs.

Puka Dog is named from the Hawaiian word "puka," which means "hole." They just put a hole into their freshly baked bread, insert the hot dog into it, and fill it in with some seriously delicious condiments. They have a lot of options on how to customize your hot dog.

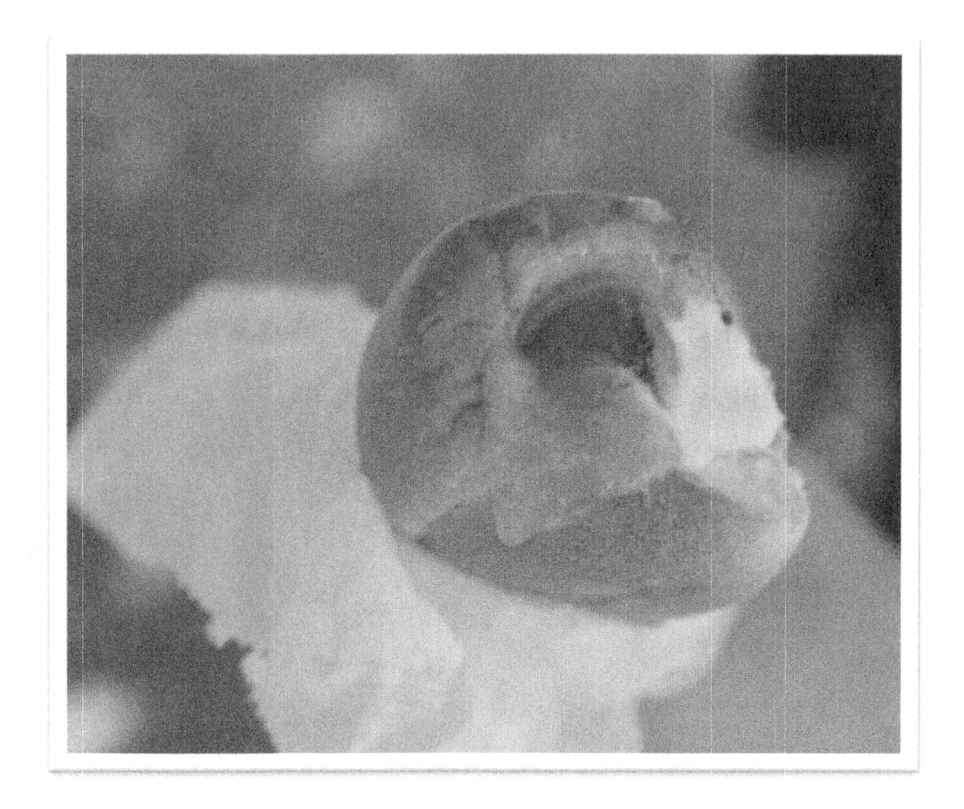

A favorite way to do it is the "Kauai Special," a spicy garlic lemon secret sauce, mango relish, and Aunty Lilikoi's passion fruit mustard. The pastries are crispy on the inside and soft on the outside.

Kiawe Roots

Whenever I ask any of my local friends or family that live on Kauai what is the best barbecue on the island, every single time, everyone says Kiawe Roots.

It is known for its smoked meat. They use kiawe wood, which is a type of mesquite, and it gives their meats a distinct and delicious flavor. The portions there are no joke. You'll get a lot of food for your money, and it will all be delicious.

Jo2 Natural Cuisine

Jo2 Natural Cuisine is a restaurant with some serious food intel. My absolute favorite thing on their menu is the poached scallop ravioli. This dish is a game-changer. It's one of those meals you'll be thinking about for weeks afterward. This dish might convert you if you're not a seafood fan.

The ravioli is made with fresh, plump scallops poached to perfection. The pasta is delicate and perfectly cooked. The sauce is light and flavorful, with a hint of lemon. The dish is finished with a sprinkling of fresh herbs.

I highly recommend going to Jo2 Natural Cuisine and ordering the poached scallop ravioli. You won't be disappointed.

Kala lea Juice Hale

If you're hunting for fresh, healthy juices on the island of Kauai, look no further than Kala lea juice hale. This unassuming juice stand offers various locally sourced, organic fruits and vegetables in their juices and smoothies.

While you might be tempted to go for the fresh juices, don't miss out on their amazing acai bowls. Made with the freshest ingredients and topped with various fruits, nuts, and granola, these bowls are the perfect pick-me-up after hiking or surfing. Trust me; you won't be disappointed.

Koloa Fish Market in Kauai

As far as fish markets go, it's one of the best. It's a no-frills, down-to-earth kind of place that's all about the fish.

The best part is you can get a whole pound of poke for a very reasonable price. So, if you're a fresh fish and poke fan, stop by the Kaloa Fish Market in Kauai.

They also have other stuff on the menu, like daily specials, plate lunches, and kalua pork. But the fish is the star here.

Kilauea Fish Market

So now you know where to get the best poke on the island. But where do you get the best fish tacos and fish burritos?

You're going to find those at the Kilauea Fish Market. The fish tacos and burritos are out of this world. And it's not just because they're made with the freshest fish you'll ever taste. The flavors are complex and vibrant, with the perfect balance of heat and acidity.

It's the kind of food that makes you want to close your eyes and savor every single bite. The fish is so fresh it practically jumps off the plate. And when you combine that with the perfectly seasoned rice, beans, and vegetables, you've got a meal that's not just ono (delicious) but also sustainable.

Konohiki Seafoods

Konohiki Seafoods is the best seafood spot in Lihue, especially if you want a quick bite to eat. It's one of the most popular seafood markets in all of Kauai. It has an awesome takeout spot in Lihue. It's known for its great selection of fish and takeout items, including handmade sushi rolls, cold Ramen, and Bento boxes. The star of the show for me at Konohiki Seafoods will be the nigiri rolls.

They have so many different things to choose from. They also offer child-size Bento boxes. Konohiki Seafoods is located relatively close to the airport, so it's a great choice if you need something quick to grab on your way or when you fly in.

Kauai Juice Company

There are locations all over the island, and many juice bars are out there these days. But what differentiates Kauai Juice Company is its commitment to using locally sourced organic produce. And let me tell you, you can taste the difference.

Their menu is full of inventive juice combinations. It's not the cheapest juice out there, but you are paying for the quality of the ingredients.

Kenji Burger

Kenji Burger is the spot to go if you like chicken katsu or burgers. And they have multiple locations on the island. I love that all of their meat is Kauai grass-fed beef. The meat is tender and flavorful; you can tell it's been raised carefully.

And if you're in the mood for something different, their chicken katsu burger is a delicious alternative. It's crispy, juicy, and packed with umami flavor. Their burgers are juicy, messy, and stacked with all the toppings you could want.

Chapter 5: Unforgettable Breakfast, Lunch, and Dinner Experiences

These are the top breakfast, lunch, and dinner locations:

Breakfast

Java Kai

For coffee enthusiasts, Java Kai has two locations on Kauai: one in Kapa'a and one in Kilauea.

Although the line at the Kapa'a location is often long, their coffee, tea, smoothies, and breakfast sandwiches make the wait worthwhile.

Wake Up Cafe

Wake Up Cafe in Hanalei is a newer breakfast spot that exclusively serves breakfast and lunch. With a retro vibe, they serve delicious breakfast items and local favorites like chili pepper chicken.

Donkey & Goat in Kapa'a

Craving Mediterranean cuisine? Donkey & Goat in Kapa'a is the place to go. Their extensive menu features various salads, sandwiches, and flatbreads.

Plantation Gardens in Lihue

Enjoy a beautiful setting and a delectable Hawaiian and American cuisine menu at Plantation Gardens in Lihue.

Hungry Portuguese in Hanapepe

For those seeking Portuguese food, The Hungry Portuguese in Hanapepe is a beloved local spot. Classic dishes like laulau to kalua pork offer a flavorful taste of Portugal.

Roy's Restaurant

Roy's Restaurant in Poipu is a popular choice for fine dining. Their Pacific Rim cuisine focuses on using fresh, locally-sourced ingredients.

Giovanni's Shrimp Truck

Don't miss Giovanni's Shrimp Truck in Hanalei, renowned for its mouthwatering garlic shrimp. They also serve other seafood dishes and refreshing acai bowls.

One Kitchen

Recently renovated and reopened, One Hanalei Bay features One Kitchen, a breakfast spot with a breathtaking view over Hanalei Bay and the mountains. Whether ordering off the menu or enjoying the breakfast buffet, the experience is worth the price.

The Old St. Regis also offers a breakfast buffet, although slightly pared down. You'll still find a selection of fresh fruit, juices, made-to-order omelets, an assortment of donuts and rolls, and waffles with various syrups, capturing the essence of a high-end resort buffet.

Lunch

After a morning spent on an exciting excursion or exploring a captivating trail, it's natural to feel hungry and crave a delicious lunch.

So, where should you go for the best options?

Let's explore some recommendations:

Tacos Al Pastor

Located in the food truck area in Kapaa, Tacos Al Pastor offers a delightful menu with numerous tasty choices.

I recommend their fish tacos, typically made with mahi-mahi or the day's fresh catch. Opt for two tacos accompanied by a side of beans, rice, guacamole, and a chip, and you'll be treated to an amazing meal. As you savor your food, take in the ocean view 50 yards away, feel the salty air on your skin, and watch the waves crash against the shoreline.

Kilauea Fish Market

Situated in the Old Stone Mall in Kilauea, Kilauea Fish Market is a must-visit spot for seafood lovers. If you're seeking exceptional fish dishes during your time in Kauai, this is the place to go. Their ahi wraps, fish tacos, and fish plates are all fantastic options. Everything is cooked fresh on-site, so while receiving your order may take a little time, the flavors are well worth the wait. Don't miss out on their renowned sauce, a delectable blend of homemade teriyaki and sesame ginger dressing known as "The Love Potion."

Hanalei Gourmet

For a quick lunch bite, while enjoying the beach in Hanalei, I highly recommend Hanalei Gourmet. This establishment offers an excellent selection of fish dishes and non-fish options. Try their Gorgonzola hamburger, salads, or boiled shrimp seasoned with Old Bay. Save room for dessert and indulge in their brownie à la mode. You'll find Hanalei Gourmet in the old elementary school building, and if you visit during dinner, you may even enjoy live music.

Keoki's Paradise

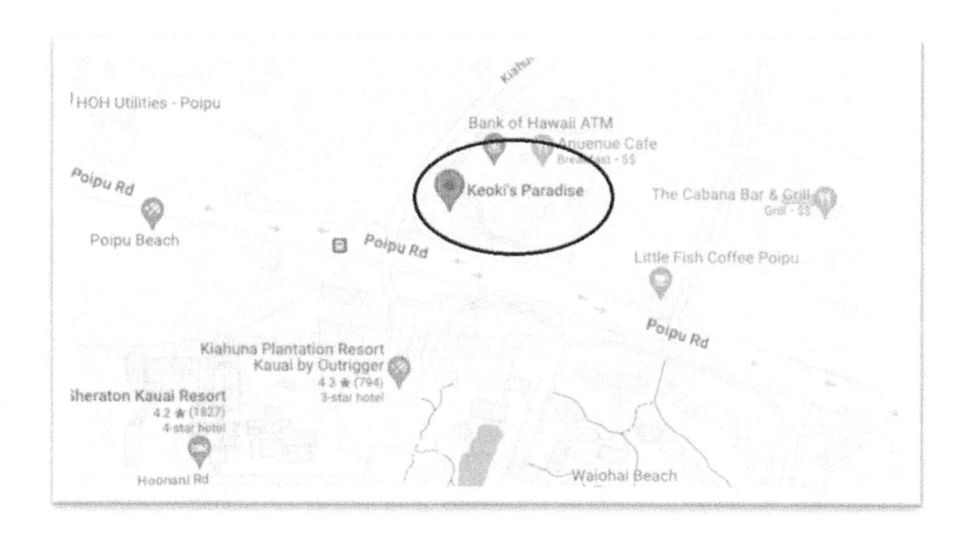

For a super fun dining experience, head to Keoki's Paradise in Kapaa. Open for both lunch and dinner, this restaurant welcomes you with a vibrant atmosphere filled with tropical plants and flowing rivers. Enjoy your drinks served in pineapple husks and explore their extensive menu, which offers a wide range of delicious options to suit every taste.

Kiawe Roots

Currently located in Kalaheo, Kiawe Roots previously operated in the Kukui Ula shopping center before relocating due to COVID. Although parking may be limited, arriving early ensures you secure a good spot.

Kiawe Roots prides itself on having a gluten-free fryer, making it an excellent choice for those with dietary restrictions. Don't miss the opportunity to try their exceptional gluten-free fried chicken and explore their menu, which features a fusion of local cuisine with a modern twist. The cafe's interior has been beautifully renovated, creating a cute, pretty, and enjoyable ambiance for your dining experience.

Dinner

Here are my top picks for dinner restaurants in Kauai:

Lavalava Beach Club in Kapaa

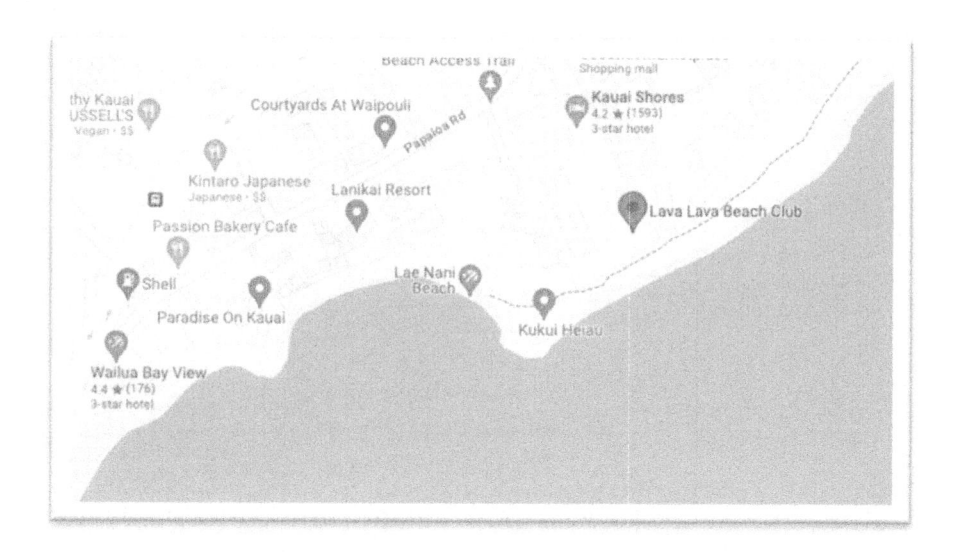

Lavalava Beach Club stands out for its beachside location. You can dine with your feet in the sand while enjoying live music. Make sure to get a reservation in advance and savor the experience of watching the waves crash against the shoreline as you listen to Hawaiian music.

Eating House 1849

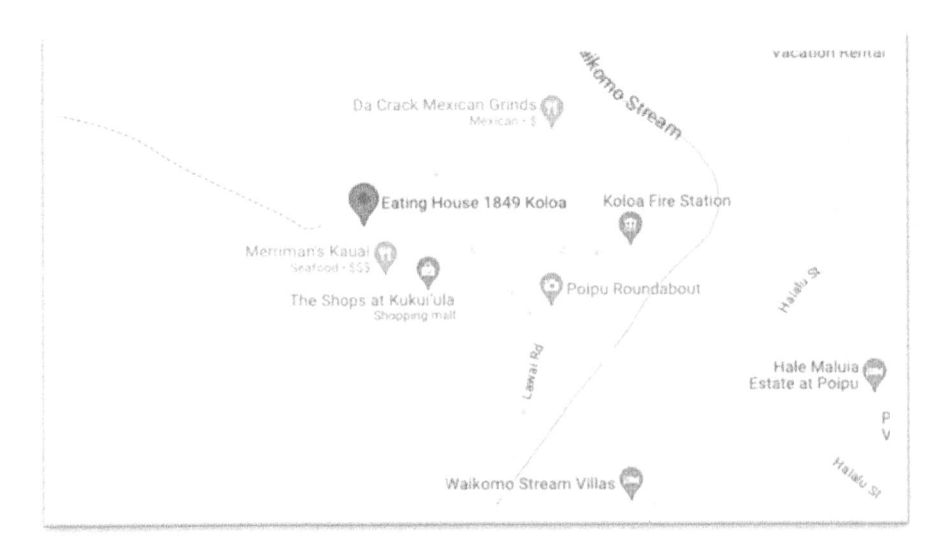

Eating House 1849 is a new restaurant concept by Roy Yamaguchi in the Kukui Ula shopping center. It celebrates the cultural fusion of Hawaii in 1849 and offers delicious dishes like seared scallops and short ribs. Don't miss their Brussels sprout appetizer and delightful drinks. If you're a fan of Roy's molten lava cake, you'll find it at Eating House 1849.

Merriman's

Considered one of the best restaurants in Hawaii, Merriman's in Kukui Ula shopping center is a popular choice. Make sure to make a reservation to secure a table. Known for using locally sourced ingredients, their macadamia nut-crusted mahi mahi is a signature dish that shouldn't be missed.

The Dolphin

The Dolphin has two locations—one in the Kukui Ula shopping center and one in Hanalei. Both offer amazing sushi and an incredible dessert called lilikoi mochi. Enjoy your meal inside, on the lanai, or in the grassy eating area along the Hanalei River.

The Dolphin doesn't take reservations, so arrive early to put your name on the list. If you or your companions aren't sushi fans, they also serve chicken and beef options.

Bar Acuda (located in Hanalei)

Bar Acuda, located in Hanalei, is one of the top dinner restaurants in Kauai. Reservations are highly recommended, as they tend to book up quickly. If you didn't make reservations, you can check for walk-in availability or sit at the bar. Bar Acuda serves its menu in tapas style, recommending three or four plates per person to share. Don't miss their popular cucumber salad, and be sure to explore their ever-changing menu that features fresh, seasonal ingredients sourced from Kauai.

Their exceptional food quality sets Bar Acuda apart from other restaurants in Kauai. It offers a dining experience that surpasses expectations.

Honorable mention restaurants:

- The Beach House in Kapaa

- Tiki Tacos in Kapaa
- Kilauea Bakery
- Slow Yourself Down in Hanalei
- Chicken in a Barrel (multiple locations around Kauai)
- Holy Grail Donuts (one in Hanalei and one in Kapaa)
- Aina Kauai in Kapaa
- Bubba's Burgers

Chapter 6: How to Save Money on a Trip to Kauai

Kauai is a captivating island renowned for its breathtaking landscapes and vibrant culture. In this chapter, I will share invaluable tips on making the most of your trip without straining your budget.

Let's delve into the best ways to save money on your upcoming visit to Kauai, ensuring you can embrace the island's allure without breaking the bank.

Be Flexible with Your Travel Dates.

Flexibility with your travel dates can be a game-changer. Similar to any popular destination, Kauai experiences peak seasons and off-peak periods. Traveling during the shoulder or off-peak seasons allows you to seize the opportunity of lower airfare and accommodation prices. Moreover, you'll relish a more serene experience on the island, avoiding the crowds and basking in the tranquility of a solitary beach. There's nothing quite like having a stretch of sand all to yourself!

Consider Alternative Accommodation

While Kauai boasts luxurious resorts that can leave you breathless, plenty of wallet-friendly alternatives exist. I recommend exploring vacation rentals, which are immensely popular on the island. Additionally, a few hostels are available for budget-conscious travelers, and camping options for those seeking a more adventurous vacation. These alternatives save you substantial money and provide a unique opportunity to immerse yourself in the island's natural beauty. If you're staying on the island's east side, particularly in Kapa'a, you'll find a hub of budget-friendly hotels. Another option to consider is utilizing Airbnb for affordable and comfortable stays.

Plan Your Meals

Plan your meals wisely through food hacking. Dining out for every single meal can quickly drain your funds. To mitigate this, I suggest taking advantage of cooking facilities in your hotel or preparing picnics to enjoy on the beach or amidst the captivating scenery of Kauai. This saves money and lets you relish the island's culinary delights while savoring its awe-inspiring vistas.

When preparing a picnic, visiting one of Kauai's vibrant farmers' markets is a fantastic option. In Kapa'a, some delightful markets offer a fun and immersive experience, allowing you to stroll through and discover incredible fresh foods. Not only is the produce undeniably fresh, but it is also reasonably priced.

Another convenient option is taking advantage of the pre-made food available at grocery stores. While many tourists flock to popular and renowned poke spots, you can find hidden gems—affordable options with generous portions—at the grocery stores. This game-changing move ensures both affordability and a satisfying meal. Additionally, while at the grocery store, you can pick up other snacks and treats to complete your picnic experience. If saving money is a priority, this is certainly a great way to do so.

Explore the Island's Wonders for Free.

Kauai has many magnificent attractions, ranging from the awe-inspiring Waimea Canyon to the idyllic beaches such as Poipu and Hanalei Hanalei Pier in the North at Princeville. These breathtaking sites allow you to appreciate the island's beauty without spending a dime. I recommend lacing up your hiking boots and embarking on some of the most captivating trails that will amaze you.

Depending on where you're staying, each island region offers unique experiences and free activities.

Free or Discounted Activities

Take advantage of free or discounted activities from tour companies or local organizations. Watch for opportunities to engage with the local community and participate in unique experiences without straining your budget. These can include cultural performances, beach cleanups, or hiking groups.

Rent a Car Strategically

Strategic car rentals can help you save money. Renting a car provides the ultimate freedom to explore Kauai at your own pace. However, the costs can add up over time. A car is essential when visiting Kauai, as the bus system may not offer the flexibility and convenience you desire. With a car, you can catch stunning sunrises and be free to do as you please.

Consider renting a car through 'Turo.' This platform allows you to choose the make, model, and color of your car and negotiate the price with the owner. You can arrange for the owner to pick you up from the airport, ensuring a seamless experience without waiting in line or unexpected fees.

You can rent a car for only a portion of your trip to save money. If you want to explore Waimea Canyon and the North Shore while staying in the South Shore, rent a car for those specific days and return it once you're done. During the remaining days, when you're primarily on the South Shore, you can forgo the car and enjoy the beaches, walk around the neighborhood, or use alternative transportation options like Uber. Be strategic in deciding which days you truly need a car to reach your desired destinations. Uber can be a cost-effective alternative for shorter distances within a specific region.

If you rent a Tesla, there is a Supercharger in Poipu on the island's south side. This can help charge your vehicle while exploring the area, providing additional convenience.

Embrace the Local Culture

Kauai is steeped in a rich cultural heritage, and there are often free or low-cost events that showcase traditional music, dance, and crafts. By immersing yourself in the local culture, you enhance your experience and discover a more authentic and budget-friendly way to connect with the island.

During my visit to Kauai, I was delighted to witness an abundance of hula dancing and hear the warm greeting of

"Aloha" everywhere I went. I made it a point to absorb the culture as much as possible. By actively participating in these opportunities, such as watching the mesmerizing hula dances or listening to Hawaiian music on the beach, you can embrace these enriching experiences at no cost. Not only will it make your journey more beautiful and authentic, but it will also add an extra layer of excitement to your adventure. There are countless creative ways to enjoy the island for free, allowing you to maximize your time on Kauai without straining your budget.

By taking advantage of these opportunities, you can fully immerse yourself in the vibrant local culture of Kauai while keeping your expenses minimal. Embrace the free events, enjoy the traditional dances, and soak in the enchanting sounds of Hawaiian music. These experiences will be memorable and provide a deeper connection to the island and its people. Kauai offers numerous avenues to enjoy its offerings without spending a fortune, making your journey all the more rewarding.

Conclusion

Kauai is a captivating island waiting to be explored and appreciated in all its splendor.

Some ways to save money while you're on Kauai are to:

- be flexible with your travel dates,
- consider alternative accommodations,
- plan your meals wisely,
- explore free attractions,
- take advantage of free or discounted activities,
- rent a car strategically, and
- embrace the local culture.

All these things will make your Kauai adventure affordable and also unforgettable.

Thank you for reading, and may your trip to Kauai be filled with beautiful memories.